Things You Can Do To HAVE A STRONGER FAMILY

SCOTT SEIDLER

CONCORDIA PUBLISHING HOUSE · SAINT LOUIS

3558 S. Jefferson Ave., St. Louis, MO 63118-3968
1-800-325-3040 · www.cph.org

Manufactured in the United States of America

1 2 3 4 5 6 7 8 9 10 22 21 20 19 18 17 16 15 14 13

TABLE OF CONTENTS

There are no perfect families. Even if things are generally okay, often there is that nagging sense your family could be better, stronger. Or maybe that domestic engine of yours feels like it's not firing on all cylinders. Take this book as an opportunity for a household tune-up. "Rattle, rattle, thunder, clatter . . ." went the old car repair commercial. For many of us, that could be the advertisement for life with our spouse, kids, and extended family members as real-life realities press in upon our spirits, tax our souls, deplete our emotions, weary our bodies, and cause us frequent feelings of futility in our own households. With exceptional ease we could simply roll over, lay down, or stick our head in the backyard sandbox. But as the apostle Paul reminded young Timothy, "God gave us a spirit not of fear but of power and love and self-control" (2 Timothy 1:7). The power and perseverance God has placed at our disposal knows only fight for, never flight from, the struggles of Christian households.

Cracked, broken, and even bombed-out families are redeemable. With God's powerful Spirit working mightily in us, "we know that for those who love God all things work together for good" (Romans 8:28). As Christians who believe in the powerful Easter victory Christ won over death, evil, and all its debilitating effects, we rejoice in Paul's confession that "in the Lord your labor is not in vain" (1 Corinthians 15:58). Ever. Period. Our efforts to live life and love others while firmly rooted in our Christian convictions always bear fruit. If Jesus Christ is the vine, we are living branches, no matter how sapped or sullied we are by the grief and dirt of this world (John 15). Therefore, we abide Him and He in us. That True Vine is our only hope.

Let a new chapter begin. In fact, let five new chapters begin. Each of the chapters that follow allow for fresh growth to emerge in our family garden. As you read, enjoy God's rich mercies, which are "new every morning" (Lamentations 3:23). Note how that promise comes from a book whose very title expresses the often-exiled feeling we experience from members of our own families. In Lamentations, the family of God, the Israelite nation, was falling apart at the seams. Yet, for our families as for that one, every day is a new day for a new kind of family to be birthed in your Christian home. Sometimes that new birth goes smoothly. Sometimes the pain almost causes us to give up and call it quits midway through delivery.

God made families the foundation of the human species. They are precious in His sight. You are precious in God's sight—so is your spouse, your kids, and your aging parents. Most of all, for the purposes of this moment, *you* are precious. You have purpose. "I know the plans I have for you, declares the LORD, plans for welfare and not for evil, to give you a future and a hope" (Jeremiah 29:11). Your family's strength and welfare is paramount in God's heart and mind. While it refers specifically to our Lord's jealous regard for His

Father's temple, applying Christ's sentiment in John 2:17 to your Christian home isn't a stretch: "Zeal for Your house will consume Me."

In the next several chapters, we'll take stock of God's divine nature expressed in three persons—Father, Son, and Holy Spirit—with the goal of aligning our family-focused efforts with His family-fortifying identity. We'll consider the significance of living as creedal creatures, as Christians who clearly value the way God shows Himself to us. We will celebrate creation and the Creator who fashioned us personally with unique personality thumbprints. This respect for our created identity helps us separate out what is truly sinful from what was once really good and God pleasing. We'll revisit the core Christian commitment to forgiveness and refresh that teaching for twenty-first-century family living. It's one thing to speak conceptually about sin in broad brushstrokes. Walking the talk of Law and Gospel and distinguishing it in real time presents countless challenges. Thankfully, we can count on God's Holy Spirit to empower us for that Law and Gospel lifestyle.

Additionally, in welcoming the Holy Spirit, we'll consider the once-in-a-lifetime opportunities that greet us each day as individuals. As the great passage from Ephesians 2:10 declares to grace-saved Christians, "We are [God's] workmanship, created in Christ Jesus for good works, which God has prepared beforehand, that we should walk in them." These Spirit-inspired works animate life inside the family. Even more, those works done by family members outside the Christian home find additional propulsion from within the Christian home.

Finally, after all that talk about doing, we'll end on a note of rest, recognizing that for all our efforts, the most important activity really involves no effort at all. Resting in what God does for you through Christ, recognizing through faith God's superceding effort to strengthen our families during Christian worship—this must be a priority in any Christian home. Christianity without resting in worship can hardly be called Christianity. Christians by definition are made for worship. To go further, Christians living by faith in God are worship in action. Fortifying this Christian faith in the rites, rituals, and rhythms of Christian liturgy is critical.

Are you ready for a stronger family? Maybe. Maybe not. The spirit may be willing, but our flesh, the actual courage to make those changes, may waver. A father once doubted anything could change his family situation. For him, the problem wasn't simply relational tension with his wife and kids. Rather, catastrophe had struck through the demon-possession of his son. The father was at a complete loss for what effort to expend personally. Even worse, the pastors and church leaders of his day gave no real help either. Coming to the Lord Jesus, the father said, " 'If You can do anything, have compassion on us and help us.' And Jesus said to him, ' "If you can"! All things are possible for one who believes.' Immediately the father of the child cried out and said, 'I believe; help my unbelief!' " (Mark 9:22–24).

Maybe for you this journey begins with that same cry of faith, "I believe; help my unbelief!" Maybe you have just about given up the fight, turned to hang up the cleats, and reached for the towel so you can throw it in and call it quits. Wait. Let's at least start the journey. Then, incrementally, patiently, through the pages of this book, we'll pause at points to make sure we haven't lost any travelers from the wagon. For now, buckle up and prepare yourself for an adventure. As Jesus said, "All things are possible for one who believes" (v. 23).

1

Jessica watched as the bus rattled off with eight-year-old Tyler safely inside. His immediate future consisted of a seven-hour school day. Her husband, Jacob, had left an hour or so earlier, wanting to start the workweek off well. Ten hours of meetings and task management would pass before he would see his family again. As for Jessica, she was somewhere between her mascara and lipstick, trying to figure out how to get her family on the same page. Despite her day job, Jessica's real preoccupation would be worrying about her family. These three lives of the Schroeder family barreled ahead at breakneck speed. By day's end the stress for everyone was palpable, concentrated in Jessica's lower back, Jacob's throbbing temple, and Tyler's restless bedtime routine.

On the other side of town, Jacob's white knuckles choked the steering wheel as he pulled into the parking lot. The traffic getting to work wasn't nearly as packed as the next three hours of his office schedule would be. The sales quarter was coming to an end, and his numbers lagged his self-determined target. Ongoing fifty-five hour workweeks hadn't yielded the income his household required to cover the credit card debt slowly creeping north. In addition, his third-grader's baseball season started two weeks ago, requiring a new uniform, bat, and glove. Each day life presented expenses his checking account couldn't cover. With his last sip of coffee before exiting the car, Jacob thought, "Is this what the next thirty-five years of life will be for me . . . for my family?"

In another part of town, Tyler could see his elementary school coming into view. His stomach grumbled. He missed his dad, wished his mom could join him for breakfast, and was tired of running from one activity to another with his friends and their parents. As the doors of the bus opened, Tyler walked into the school where the shape of his life would be formed by others for the next seven hours or so. Like a typical child, Tyler was oblivious to the forces shaping his life and preparing him for a fate similar to his parents (or worse) in adulthood.

With disciples of ages past, this family threesome cries out, "Save us, Lord" (Matthew 8:25). Their words sometimes take the form of tears, sometimes the shape of expressionless zombies while watching television to wind down, and other times a confused place in between. Whatever the form or shape, the sentiment is deep-seated. This family boat is threatening to capsize, and someone needs to intervene. By God's grace in Christ, someone will intervene.

Everyone wants a strong family. Even if they don't know how to look for it, ask for it, maybe even try for it, the desire to have a strong family lives at every altar when marriage vows are spoken. In fact, at the very heart of every human being sits the need—the deep, deep need—to belong to others and be nurtured by them. From the earliest moments of creation, the very first hours, we hear God Himself say the words that give birth to human family: "It is not good that the man should be alone" (Genesis 2:18). Genesis 1 impresses upon us that only God is good. For man to appreciate that divine goodness, our heavenly Father created a human family out of nothing by the end of chapter 2. In the context of a family, whether by marriage or by birth, and sometimes both, we can experience the strong love of God shared in the gentle warmth of human relationships.

At heart Jessica, Jacob, and Tyler all long for the same thing—belonging. Though expressed with different kinds of hopes and attached to different kinds of words, these three share the same impulse to give and receive love from one another. Sin in us frustrates those hopes. Evil around us dashes God's good intentions on the rocks of futility. Family homes can be awfully futile-feeling places these days. Borrowing on the pessimistic feel of Ecclesiastes, we may find ourselves muttering, "All things are full of weariness; . . . What has been is what will be, and what has been done is what will be done, and there is nothing new under the sun" (1:8–9). Even while reading this, you may find yourself visiting those futility-filled locations in your own family. You may be wondering and muttering, "What's the point? Why go to all the trouble of trying to change the family I feel stuck with?"

We can survive though. Lots of families are making it through the toughest and most desperate of times. They survive, often unintentionally, because they lace themselves to some thread of God's design for us as human beings. For some, this design alignment comes through family members' deep-seated appreciation for another's unique, albeit sometimes irritating, personality. Gratefulness for the quirky individuals that constitute our family is a real blessing. Others have tethered themselves to a family value of apology and forgiveness when wrongs are committed. Law and Gospel, sin and grace, lived, experienced, and managed with mercy at home is powerful. Still other families find strength supporting one another in the various callings and vocations God has given them. Christians know that our children, along with every adult human, are possessors of a vocation in which they can live vibrantly their faith in Jesus Christ. For big and small, being part of a family is a vocation; it is joyful work given to us to do.

In that threefold description—of appreciation for creation, forgiveness, and purpose in our callings—you should sense an overlap with the structure of the Christian creeds. Creation, redemption, and sanctification, the work of Father, Son, and Holy Spirit, provide families a ground of divine strength flowing from accurate identification of human weakness. Through the rest of this book, we'll consider these various threads by which God cultivates strong followers and through them strong families. Created by God, you are built both to be blessed and to be a blessing as a family. Redeemed by Jesus Christ, the power of sin and evil in you has been broken, the hope for renewed and always-renewable relationships restored. Led by the Holy Spirit, you live with purpose for the works He has prepared in advance for you to walk in—works worked with family members cheering you on and helping you out.

At the same time, beware of another approach to strengthening families practiced by millions. Calling to mind a restaurant salad bar helps illustrate this haphazard approach. There's nothing quite like the anticipation of standing in front of a restaurant buffet or salad bar when hunger rumbles inside you. Taking in all that food overwhelms our senses. And so begins that gastronomical dance: a waltz around the lettuce, a two-step toward the chicken, followed by a foxtrot in the direction of the sundae bar. Do-si-do by the drink station and then curtsy as you sit at your table. Heaven will surely include a smorgasbord at every dinner! Can you say "Seconds, anyone?"

It seems that many families take a salad bar kind of approach to strengthening their homes. A morsel of insight from a well-regarded author feeds our need to improve this week. After the hoped-for habit falls into disuse, however, we catch a tidbit of advice from a television personality interviewing a family therapist. A family meeting later, every member of the home creates action steps by which to change the domestic culture. This change doesn't seem to last either. Such a feast or famine method of family development can continue indefinitely with little likelihood of long-term impact.

Changing patterns of behavior takes effort. With God's empowering help, we can ensure our motivation, ability, family, friends, and life situation all align to help us make a real change. When God through Holy Baptism conquers the absolute power of sin in us, we are afforded the daily opportunity to live life in harmony with His commandments. Practically speaking, though, this aligned living with God's holy will takes place in heart, community, and environment. Let's look at some basic foundations for change that we cannot take for granted if we are to sustainably strengthen our Christian home.

Personal Motivation

What is your vision of your family twenty years from now? Can you narrate the experience of yourself and your kids twenty years older than you are today? Who are you and who are they? What are you all doing at that moment? What does your holiday get-together look like? How are your grandchildren behaving? What is going on with great-grandpa? What goes into the table prayer? What about the cribside prayers that are said? Being able to describe that vision helps refocus the current places that cause you the greatest angst. If you picture your two daughters behaving like sane, self-giving adult sisters someday, then you have a clearer picture of what efforts need to be central now. In other words, all the anxiety about messy rooms or on-time homework is not nearly as important as honing the interpersonal quality of your home.

This personal motivation cannot be limited to one person in a household alone. Unless everyone is on the same page with wanting to improve life within and outside the home, little will likely change. The same exercise must be put to use by as many members of the family as possible. Without a shared passion for a brighter future, we return once again to that dreaded salad bar. Everyone chooses what seems right in his or her own eyes, yet no one agrees that what any one person is doing really is worthwhile for everyone else to try.

A great way to get everyone in the family on the same page is through regular family devotions. Consider using *Portals of Prayer, My Devotions, Little Visits with God* (and others in that series), or any of the other wonderful resources available for families.

Personal Skills

Beyond motivation, that hope for the future that impacts our behavior today, is the necessary question of capacity. Given what you want to see, do you have the ability to bring that vision to reality? Be honest.

Brad's two preteen daughters fought tooth and nail every morning in the bathroom. Sometimes their words dripped with poison. Brad yelled at the kids, counseled them, begged them, and ignored them. Nothing worked. "Maybe this is the best I can expect," Brad reasoned.

Later that day at work, one of the people who worked under Brad came into Brad's cube needing some assistance on a project. What was a sincere request for help, not much different from being asked to share a blow-dryer, earned a stinging piece of sarcasm and a condescending response from Brad. Brad, however, was clueless about how he came off to his co-worker. Not surprisingly, his co-worker took a job with another company three weeks later.

Preteenagers can't go work for another company or put an advertisement in the paper for new parents. One of the most critical responsibilities of parents seeking to strengthen their home is to live by the proverb of Socrates to "know thyself." For what ails their home, parents must first appreciate their own limitations and skill shortfalls.

Returning to Brad's story, after a stunning year-end performance review led to a required class on conflict resolution and interpersonal skill improvement, things improved dramatically both at work and at home. Brad listened and spoke with his daughters differently, more openly. Soon, the ferocity of the morning bathroom battle lessened. The girls still acted like girls sharing a bathroom—human nature can only change so much in adolescence! In regard for each other's needs, however, the girls changed for the better.

In this example there was no grandiose plan or big-family-meeting-induced change. Brad simply acquired an interpersonal skill set that changed the dynamic of the family and caused him to behave differently. He cultivated a different kind of soil for his family to grow stronger in and blossom more brightly.

The skills that Brad acquired bled over into the lives of his daughters. They didn't attempt to do anything new consciously. Brad's personal skill change became an environmental change that caught his daughters unawares. Without even knowing it, the two girls felt something different was at work in the house.

Social Setting

Families are surrounded. Like settlers on the prairie or an army in enemy territory, every family lives with social supporters or antagonists. Maximizing your support and minimizing the antagonism is critical to successfully strengthening your home. Look around your family, outside of it. Who are your closest friends? What about the kids and parents closest to your children? Do these people provide a net-plus or a net-minus to your family's health and well-being?

Sarah loved lunchtime at her office. It was a great opportunity to break away from the grind of the accounting/audit department. The two other ladies she worked with came from similar places in life. They raised kids the same age as Sarah and lived in similar neighborhoods. Sarah enjoyed the time she spent with them because she felt like they "got" her. Listening into the conversation, however, helps us to see exactly what she was getting.

Tamara and Ellen were Sarah's co-workers and best friends at the office. Tamara incessantly shared stories on her husband's lack of follow-through on even the simplest of housework. She was a great storyteller and, so, her tales of tortured home-life were hilarious. Ellen's teenage son and daughter, according to Ellen's analysis, attempted to outdo each other in terms of how awful their bedrooms could become. Humorous in a way, Ellen's constant critique of her children made Sarah feel better about the normalcy of her own offspring.

Yet, unknown to Sarah, there was a price being paid for listening to these friends. That price was increasing hopelessness that anything could change and encouragement to complain about minor problems in her own family. Funny as they were, Sarah didn't realize that with every passing story her optimism for the improvement of her family's situation declined. Tamara and Ellen were good people. As friends, they would be there for Sarah in a pinch. However, they were not true allies in Sarah's effort to strengthen her family. Rather, Sarah's two co-workers had become unknowing accomplices in weakening it.

We absolutely must assess who in our world serves as allies or antagonists to our aspirations for change. Direct challenge to our change efforts or snide remarks made in passing can cripple our motivation or undercut the sustainability of efforts to increase our personal skill set. Antagonists take the air out of our balloon and lessen the likelihood that our families can rise from the ash heap of futility once again.

Environmental Hazards

One hundred sixty-eight. That is the number of hours each of us have at our disposal weekly. Assuming that fifty-six of those hours are used for the necessary eight hours of good sleep nightly, we are left with one hundred twelve to use as we see fit. The stewardship of those hours for a typical American is not good. Figure at least eight hours consuming food. Tack on another forty in work or school. That leaves us with discretionary time totaling sixty-four hours. At first glance, that amount of time seems huge. But don't forget twenty-four of them are used by most kids in front of a television. Then, consider all that may yet be calculated in: family time, conversations with friends, hygiene, homework, housework, yardwork, sports, and driving to and from everywhere we're going. By the time we're done, most of us feel lucky to have even an hour a day to spend on "less urgent" matters, including, unfortunately, strengthening our families.

How will you move heaven and earth in order to strengthen your family? With all these competing pressures for your time, you probably have already felt the pinch of making space for intentionally strengthening your family. Beyond the social power of helpers and antagonists, the culture we live in impels us to make choices that often lead to unintended consequences.

Nine-year-old Alex was going to be a soccer star who rode through his college days on a sports scholarship—at least that was the sugarplum vision of his parents. In order to accomplish this, Al played soccer twice as much as his elementary school counterparts. Literally. He participated in the school team after classes ended, ate a quick dinner (fast food), and then trucked over to the indoor soccer park where his select team played.

The parental justification for this had grown since the lad began soccer in preschool. At first, his parents' reasoning held that soccer was good for socialization. Then came the logic that Alex's continued participation would provide him with a kind of stick-to-itiveness benefiting him in later life. As college years came on the horizon, the idea of a free and full tuition ride emerged. Pretty soon, still more arguments arose as family members questioned the freakish time commitments being made so that little Alex might become a supersized American Pele chasing a Brandi Chastain monumental moment in the Olympics. Alas, parental optimism springs eternal.

But don't forget Alex's younger sister and brother, five-year-old Alexa and one-year-old Colin. Their extracurricular futures may be just as bright as that of their older brother.

The father of three children myself (none of whom play soccer well), I am exhausted by this vision. But anyone who knows this theme can recite countless variations on it. Replace school soccer for band and select soccer for after-school clarinet lessons and you may find yourself in the same boat.

You see, the structures of our lives, the commitments we have made, and the cultural expectations that govern us—these outside and impersonal forces kill healthy families. To be blunt, they are murderous, especially when paired with accomplices (see social setting above) who only exaggerate the deficiencies in our personal motivation and skill at making positive and constructive change in our lives.

The Apostles' Creed focuses on the work of our God, Father, Son, and Holy Spirit, and helps us bring these often-antagonistic forces under an understandable and helpful governing structure. The Creed shapes our understanding of God as He intersects with daily life. Helpfully, this God is "for us" in every way possible. Appreciating His identity assists us in planning how to strengthen our families, while neutralizing the negative effects of personal deficiencies, social pressure, and structural chaos.

Regarding the person and work of our Father Creator, families grow stronger the more they appreciate the created identity of each member and the unique contribution each family member brings to the whole of humanity. Regarding the person and work of Christ the Savior, families grow stronger the more they courageously confess sin to one another and freely forgive one another. Regarding the person and work of the sanctifying Holy Spirit, families grow stronger the more they encourage and bolster each other's specific vocations, their God-given mission fields for seeking and saving the lost through word and action.

To bolster your family in a more active way, consider using CPH's *Family Faith Walks*, which combines devotions, activities, and family excursions. A great resource for group events in your church or school is CPH's *Funtastic Family Nights*, which encourages fellowship, active learning, and family discussion.

The remainder of this book chronicles the impact God, the Father, Son, and Holy Spirit, has on our families because of the unique work of each person of the Godhead. Heady stuff, to be sure. However, rest assured that ours is not a God who cannot be fathomed or known. Rather, God wants to be known and is, in fact, dedicated to being known by those He has created and loved with an eternal love. That's you! From here on out, hope increases with every page that follows. Hope increases because, by God's grace, the following pages are filled with doxology. They are filled with an ever-expanding hymn of praise to the God who formed our families before the creation of the world and has written our names through Baptism in the book of life, which leads us to the world that is to come.

Key Points

- Families grow stronger as they align themselves with the work of God as expressed in the Apostles' Creed.
- Strong families address the changing patterns of family and personal behavior that weigh upon a family.
- God is pro-family. If He is for us, we know there is always another chance to change our families for the better.

Discussion Questions

Consider these words from Martin Luther's introduction to the Apostles' Creed in the Large Catechism:

The Creed . . . sets forth to us everything that we must expect and receive from God. To state it quite briefly, the Creed teaches us to know Him fully. This is intended to help us do what we ought to do according to the Ten Commandments. For . . . the Ten Commandments are set so high that all human ability is far too feeble and weak to keep them. Therefore, it is just as necessary to learn this part of Christian doctrine as to learn the former. Then we may know how to attain what they command, both where and how to receive such power. For if we could by our own powers keep the Ten Commandments as they should be kept, we would need nothing further, neither the Creed nor the Lord's Prayer. (II 1–3)

1. What have you determined your household, your family, most needs to receive from God? Merciful and kind attitudes toward one another? Commitment to follow through on tasks? Compassion? Direction in how to live for others?

2. What prevents you from believing optimistically that your family situation can change? Years of backsliding from the love that first brought you and your spouse to the altar? The overcommitted lifestyle you are leading? Financial stress that grips every activity the family does?

3. What one-sentence prayer can become your fellow traveler as you begin the journey of strengthening your family? Take a moment and in a single, concise sentence express to God what desire is at the heart of your soul when it comes to the strengthening of your family.

4. With what other family members are you reading this book? "Misery loves company" not just because someone listens to another's sad plight. The phrase "Misery loves company" reminds us that the fellowship of other compassionate human beings ensures the overcoming of that defeated spirit. Who are your Christian counterparts in this journey, your social allies who will pray, prod, and proclaim for you the great promises of God that greet every Spirit-filled step?

Action Items

1. As they are able, have each family member talk about how he or she hopes your family could grow stronger. Invite little children to draw and describe two pictures: one depicting your family as it currently stands and the other depicting what a "better" family would look like. Hang these descriptions and pictures on your refrigerator or another prominent location to keep the vision of a stronger family constantly before your eyes.

2. Identify another person or couple in your congregation—ideally an older adult who has made it through some family struggles and lived to tell about—you can confide in and draw on for support.

3. Talk with your pastor and other wise church members about starting a family-centered Bible study or fellowship group. Nurture this group as a place for families to bring their feelings of futility and to find strength to fight through this toward health and vitality.

I believe in God, the Father Almighty, Maker of heaven and earth.

What does this mean?

I believe that God has made me and all creatures; that He has given me my body and soul, eyes, ears, and all my members, my reason and all my senses, and still takes care of them. He also . . . richly and daily provides me with all that I need to support this body and life. He defends me against all danger and guards and protects me from all evil. All this He does only out of fatherly, divine goodness and mercy, without any merit or worthiness in me. (Small Catechism, First Article)

Remember well: the fruit is not the tree. Sometimes the fruit falls close. Sometimes it falls further away. The truth, however, remains that every human being differs from every other. Both body and soul differ from human to human. Senses, emotions, and mental faculties all differ too. Strong families recognize no two pieces of fruit are the same—they come in different shapes, sizes, and positions. Getting comfortable with the notion that your children are not you is often a parent's hardest task. Though they might be similar to either of you, your kids are not cut from exactly the same cloth as either you or your spouse, so no blaming your soulmate for qualities you don't like. Coming to grips with the reality that your spouse's personality traits are here to stay is sometimes the most stressful realization of a young marriage. It can be similarly stressful to accept the personality traits of your children.

Reconciling yourself with your Creator's creative decisions is a top priority as a child of God. God makes no mistakes when it comes to fashioning exactly the kind of human being He wants from the womb. Experiences and the like may push a human being in one direction or another, and in life we all have choices to make. But accepting the foundational truth that God is the author of every human life takes great faith and fortitude. It takes faith to believe He is truly the Creator who makes all things out of nothing. It takes fortitude to accept that what He made was truly intentional and at heart a good idea.

What's more, all of those created senses, reason, and mental faculties that combine to form an individual's personality traits are not to be understood as personality flaws. Traits differentiate things. Flaws destroy things and are the result of sin at work in us. Traits do not by definition make life difficult. Flawed human beings do that. That said, the frustrating narrative of differing personality traits in action repeats itself with so many variations. Consider these cases:

— the dad whose high school athletic glory will never be relived in his literature-loving son

— the mom whose social ease finds little reflection in her introverted daughter

— the son whose need for an affirming word has little hope for fulfillment from his strong, silent father

— the daughter whose looks and popularity unsettle her book-smart mother who didn't learn how to put on makeup until college

None of the above indicate any flaw in these human beings. Each of these stories, though, is indicative of many competing personality traits. Competition in traits can breed frustration between people. Given time, personality-based frustration can lead to condemnation, exclusion, and hatred. Think about the person who seemingly never violated one of the Ten Commandments in your presence yet nevertheless drives you absolutely batty. You can't put your finger on why the person infuriates you with every social interaction; he or she just does. Maybe the problem is not the other person. Maybe the problem is not you either. It takes two to tango. Maybe the problem is the intersection of your personalities.

When Personalities Collide

Drawing on the vignettes above, especially the last snippet about beauty and intellect, consider this extended story.

Haley intimidated Diane. Even though Haley was only fifteen, she had all the earmarks of intellectual brilliance. A great GPA in high school derived from an almost uncanny ability to understand most every academic subject easily. Homework never accompanied Haley home. In fact, Haley read that as irony—her homework was really her schoolwork. She plowed through it in high school academic lab (study hall for the GenX and Boomer crowd). Though Diane knew she should simply be proud of her daughter, Diane struggled with a guilt-ridden life.

Growing up, Diane lacked most of the resources for success Haley now had. She was born and raised in a hard-working family who prized education but never excelled in it. Through sheer effort, after starting as a teller nineteen years earlier, Diane had earned a good-paying job at a bank that afforded Haley great opportunities. The problem was that in many ways Diane and Haley no longer spoke the same language, even though they lived in the same house.

Diane, you see, had made the choice to keep working while Haley was growing up. Dedicating well over forty hours each week to a place where her daughter could not come, Diane wondered if part of that perceived distance came because of her career choice. In reality, the answer was probably both yes and no. For Diane, though, the answer was entirely a loud yes.

Now, Haley wanted to attend an excellent school—one that would prize her academic success. She wanted to see the world, escape smaller town limitations, and explore all that God had made. The more Haley dreamed and talked and dreamed some more, the more Diane felt like she was losing her already-lost daughter. They argued about which colleges to visit. While Haley felt her family chains holding her back, Diane reasoned the regional university was good enough for any future. What Diane could not reason through was a healthy conclusion for this relational mess.

Such tales of "whoa!" can cause any of us to marvel that families can get along with each other at all! But families can thrive, for God has given us this ability as part of His perfect human plan. Consider this: because God made each of us different, we have no hope of birthing or rearing an exact match to ourselves, an identical twin of personality and personal ability. That daughter you reckon got dropped off by an alien spaceship—she's God's handiwork. That son who vexes your every decision—he's God's wonderful creation.

I had a conversation last week with one of my colleagues at the congregation I pastor. She told the story of the ferocious arguments that colored the relationship she had with her oldest son. This mom recalled one particular argument in which she realized after several minutes that the position she had been defending was now being defended by her son. Somewhere in the middle of the debate, he had determined to argue her position without informing her. In legal terms, he became a hostile witness against himself! When she realized her son's self-betrayal, she called him out on his flip-flop, only to have him retort, "Yeah, I saw your point and knew you were right, but I didn't want to tell you, so I just decided to argue against me with you."

Spawn of the devil? No. That's just your kid. And he is precious in God's sight. With wonderful warmth, as she tells the story, the twinkle in her eye tells you her son is as precious in her sight as the day she first held him in her arms.

To learn more about how personality differences affect families, check out David Ludwig's *Renewing the Family Spirit* (St. Louis: Concordia, 1989).

Look, it's not about being the same. It's about the identity of our Creator God uniquely creating each human being for His purposes. The challenge is to embrace the differences as God-authored opportunities to more fully appreciate Him, the Creator of all creatures. Instead of being antagonized by what our kids, spouse, or other family members are—their personalities, predispositions, and proclivities—the invitation from the Creator is to enjoy them, receive them with thanksgiving, and encourage their continued development.

The Creator's Good Gifts

Let's reflect a moment on this by diving deeper into the Church's teaching on the First Article of the Creed. As mentioned in chapter 1, this Christian creed gives us a shape by which to view our world and understand the way our God interacts with it. The entirety of our world's history, from fantastic beginning to spectacular end and all of human experience in between, connects at every point to the person and work of God. He creates, redeems from sin, and energizes for faith-filled worship and ministry to others. Not a single moment of our lives expires without the consecrating and coordinating activity of God as He sustains, supplies, or spiritually revives it. "In Him we live and move and have our being" (Acts 17:28). Life is about Him. Our lives, every one of them and every part of them, each and every day, are in His hands. In giving glory to God, Paul writes, "For from Him and through Him and to Him are all things. To Him be glory forever. Amen" (Romans 11:36).

The very first statement of conviction of a redeemed Christian acknowledges the creative work of God. The Creed's first assertion, our First Article faith, relates the purity of creation. Sin, in other words, was nowhere yet to be found. Sin was not present when language erupted from our mouths. Think about that. Language is fundamentally a good thing. Even though we can curse God with our lips, the very use of words is not the problem. Rather, as Christ reminds us, "What comes out of a person is what defiles him. . . . All these evil things come from with, and they defile a person" (Mark 7:20, 23). Consider that when Adam and Eve were created, with their creation came unique personalities. We have these too. Personality is the way in which we express ourselves to the world because of experiences (nurture) and biological predispositions (nature). Language and personality are First Article gifts that existed in purity before evil reared its ugly head. Most of us, however, don't acknowledge this. The risk of such oversight in families is significant.

Because we don't consider fully the Creed's First Article, our tendency is to minimize the goodness of God in the gifts given there. Differing personalities become cause for spiritual judgment. Unique ways of using words or conveying thoughts receive suspect-laden critique—if not outright condemnation. Books are burned. Fires are lit. And countless lives are lost because of differences we have hastily determined are really spiritual deficiencies. They rarely are. Nevertheless, as a result, we are hard-pressed to accept differences in language and personality as anything but a problem. Racism, prejudice, and cultural elitism, among many other sin-induced -isms, are all extremes of what at heart is essentially the rejection of another for simply being different.

The thesis of this chapter challenges us to "hate the sin but love the sinner"—especially those unique, God-ordained traits that sinners bears. These traits are not essentially sinful. Sin is not the trait itself. Traits are traits. However, how we misuse those traits or abuse others with them is sinful. But the grace of God in Jesus Christ serves to overcome even this. As the apostle John reminds us, "The reason the Son of God appeared was to destroy the works of the devil" (1 John 3:8). We'll say more on Christ's salvation in a few moments.

For now, step back and take stock of the personality traits that are at work in your family. What value does the artistically disposed or the athletically inclined or the street-smart personality provide for your household? In the Creed we confess that we all are sinful and fall short of God's glory. With that creedal confession should also come the simultaneous conviction that there are some qualities in us that are neither good nor bad. These simply are what it means to be human. What are some of those qualities in your family?

Before going further, please don't misunderstand the point above. The completely corrupting power of sin ought not be misstated or misrepresented. The entirety of our being is repulsive to God because of sin and antagonistic to the other humans with whom we share this globe. But sin takes what is good from God and distorts it. Especially in terms of personality, what we have from God is good and unique, albeit now corrupted in uniquely sinful ways by sin itself. Allowing for this by faith helps us appreciate the specific corruption affecting each individual. It helps prepare us for the unique redemption and sanctification that God will effect in each of us through Christ and the powerful work of the Holy Spirit.

Adapting to Serve

Paul could be described as a flexibly rigid pastor. Rigid, unbending, and sometimes seemingly hard-hearted when it came to sin and a congregation's lack of conformity to God's will, Paul had no problem preaching the Law of God in its full terror. But that stern commitment to God's holiness was tempered by a tenderness that would shock even the most nurturing of preschool teachers! Like a gentle father, he would bend over backwards to articulate the Gospel of mercy and forgiveness. Describing his ministry, Paul contended, "I have made myself a servant to all, that I might win more of them. To the Jews I became as a Jew, in order to win Jews. To those under the law I became as one under the law. . . . To those outside the law I became as one outside the law. . . . To the weak I became weak. . . . I have become all things to all people, that by all means I might save some. I do it all for the sake of the gospel, that I may share with them in its blessings" (1 Corinthians 9:19–23).

There were certainly circumstantial adjustments Paul made to his diet or personal code of conduct—as long as God's Law was not impugned. What is equally imaginable and amazing, though, is the bending of Paul's personality to match the personality of those he shared a meal with or engaged in conversation. You can easily picture Paul's pattern of speech and demeanor changing with each changing conversation. In fact, to an extent, you see that reflected in the personality of his thirteen preserved letters. Each one bears the mark of the apostle's personality, along with an affirming nod to the cultural and personal idiosyncrasies of that letter's addressee.

Let me make one more point. Please recognize something that to this point may have easily been overlooked. Through all those years you've spent with your distinctively and divinely made child, your little angel, you have changed, too . . . for the better! Consider again Diane's situation above. Little did she appreciate how her own thinking had sharpened as she walked through science fairs and proofed history papers. Right under her nose, the very capabilities developed in her daughter had made her a more thoughtful person. True, Diane still couldn't pass a calculus test to save her life, but because of her daughter's frequent observations, she could have a conversation about statistics while listening to a news program.

Not only that, consider how Paul grew in wisdom through his years of engaging countless different sinners as they walked the road of salvation and found hope in Christ alone. Paul grew enough to leave his disciple Timothy with these poignant words: "The Lord's servant must not be quarrelsome but kind to everyone, able to teach, patiently enduring evil, correcting his opponents with gentleness. God may perhaps grant them repentance leading to a knowledge of the truth" (2 Timothy 2:24–25). For Paul and, as he hoped, for Timothy, ministry to others was not just about knowing how to deal with flaws surfaced in sin. Knowing and appreciating the unique human beings being dealt with in a spirit of gentleness was a necessary competency as well. How much more is this true for our families! While sin is present in every relationship, we start with a tremendous reason for being charitable to our families and gentle in our approach: they are our flesh and blood. Each of our kids, our parents, and especially our spouses deserve the benefit of any doubt we may have about them and their character, their ability to change, and the possibility of improved relationship with them.

Good Gifts Gone Bad

Consider this case: David's ability to cut to the chase and confront problems at work was well-known. Known as a fearless manager, his skill in weaving through tricky situations had increased through the years. That skill, however, did not stay at the office when the workday ended. His wife, Sarah, knew too well what kind of response was likely to come from him when problems arose at home. David's executive demeanor was on call 24/7. Unfortunately, sometimes problems didn't need to be solved. Sometimes fires burning on the homefront needed to be assessed and understood first before solutions were applied.

David and Sarah's two children were active in sports and all sorts of extracurriculars. Managing their jobs and their kids' calendars was becoming a nightmare. The truth was that this schedule would not be easily changed. The household needed to earn money. Kids needed to pursue their activities. What Sarah wished David knew was that she needed an ally, not an executive, for a husband.

When push came to shove at work, David had supreme confidence in his abilities. Others thought it bordered on arrogance. Both conclusions were well-placed. At home, however, that strong self-perception quickly turned the smallest problems into poisonous ones. David's talent, his spiritual gift in many ways, was leadership. But sin in David had blinded him from that wisdom and had diminished the role Sarah played in their family decisions.

As David and Sarah worked on their marriage, it took effort for both of them to value the perspectives of the other. On the one hand, it was a monumental task for David to see how his God-given, humanly honed ability to dissect a problem could present a real problem for Sarah. While never intentionally meaning to come across as domineering, his natural intuition and great joy in discovering and enacting solutions caused him to do just that. David's passion presented him as a bully. If someone found him- or herself in front of David's passion, it meant moving aside or putting up a fight.

All that said, at times David did know better. His keen intuition sometimes told him to slow down, ask more questions, and involve others in conversation. More often, though, David reasoned that solving a problem quickly was better than solving a problem together. He figured that a quick end justified David-determined means. That calculation was in many ways the rearing of sin's ugly power through David's personality. This is one example of how sin can take something that is good at heart—a mere human personality, senses, reason, and mental faculties—and completely twist it for self-centered purposes and satisfaction.

Restoring creation is the purpose and work of Jesus Christ. While we will discuss a Christian's capacity to give and receive forgiveness in the next chapter, we first need to talk about the power of forgiveness at work in a Christian. By the power of Christ's atoning death and glorious resurrection from the grave, the power of sin has been broken in us. In destroying the works of the devil, our Lord Jesus Christ also destroyed that demonic work that causes us to hate others, serve ourselves, and get completely twisted in the middle of such messy relationships. Paul writes about how Christ "Himself is our peace, who has made us both one and has broken down in His flesh the dividing wall of hostility . . . that He might create in Himself one new man in place of the two, so making peace" (Ephesians 2:14–15). While speaking specifically about how Jews and Gentiles are both reconciled to God, the underlying concept is that of unity among humanity. One Body comes of Christ's atoning work. Hands need feet need eyes need ears. Every member, every gift-mix, and every talent pool is essential. Only through Jesus Christ is this sinful divisiveness destroyed.

In touching upon the First Article of the Creed we stand at a crossroads. If we take seriously the conversation we have had, we really have hard work to do. But we can also remember the vision that because of Christ's powerful work of reconciliation, opposing personalities can be at peace with each other. While Isaiah can anticipate that "The wolf shall dwell with the lamb. . . . The nursing child shall play over the hole of the cobra, and the weaned child shall put his hand on the adder's den" (11:6, 8), we can anticipate even better among the family of God. You, too, can honor the blessing that each one of your family members is a unique creation of God.

Key Points

- Strong families recognize each member's value in light of each being a creature of God the Creator.
- Sin weakens families by diminishing how each family member views the goodness God has creatively built into the other members. Strong families resist.
- Sin weakens families as it corrupts the personalities of each member—bending them to self-satisfaction instead of self-sacrifice for the others. Strong families nurture a culture of sacrifice among their members.
- Only the restorative work of Jesus gives the power to counteract both the sinful misuse of our personalities and the sinful misjudgment of our family members' differing personalities.

Discussion Questions

1. The following categories help distinguish differing personality types in people. It's not always clear cut, but which categories match your family members best?

   — Outgoing and social/Shy and reserved

   — Lives life intuitively as if by a sixth sense/Lives life rationally, making decisions based on fact

   — Filled with feelings and emotions/Filled with thoughts and intellect

— Focused and decisive/Open-minded and as a consequence, at times, indecisive

2. When you think of these different personal qualities, which one most often irritates you? Turn the curse to a blessing by identifying what negative things would happen if that personal quality disappeared from the face of the earth. What if the world was filled with only extroverts or only logical thinkers?

3. Why are your God-given personal qualities so valuable in this world and for your family? What do you offer your family that could not easily be found in someone else? What can you do to ensure that no other part of your personality interferes with the full deployment of that personal strength, winsomely, among your family members?

Action Items

1. Go online and find a reputable personality inventory or assessment and take it as a family. Many have versions for both adults and kids. Have fun comparing and contrasting the different ways in which each family member's personality complements or frustrates others. Spend time identifying ways to encourage each other's God-given personality.

2. Get serious about your own personality flaws. Ask a close friend, co-worker, or teacher where your

personality blind spot is found. Confess the need to sand off the rough edges of your personality so that the personalities of others can really shine. Remember, we are not necessarily confessing an actual sin. Rather we are acknowledging to God what sin at work in us causes us to ignore: the fact that different people relate to life differently.

And [I believe] in Jesus Christ, His only Son our Lord . . . .

What does this mean?

I believe that Jesus Christ . . . is my Lord, who has redeemed me, a lost and condemned person, purchased and won me from all sins, from death, and from the power of the devil . . . with His holy, precious blood and with His innocent suffering and death. (Small Catechism, Second Article, p. 329)

Get used to saying "I'm sorry." Even more, get used to saying, "I forgive you."

Strong families demonstrate increasing mastery of repentance and forgiveness. Such mastery comes from a clear appreciation of what Christ accomplished for each of them on the cross and through the empty tomb of His resurrection. Because in Christ God forgives us, as our families live in the light of Christ, we forgive others. What's more, strong families are aware that this ability does not come fully honed when a bride and groom arrive at the altar. It is not a spiritual aptitude that develops overnight, nor does there exist a future day when one's work in this area of Christian character will be complete. Repentance and forgiveness is a lifelong part of our daily devotion to Jesus Christ. From Baptism to final Christian breath, the arduous yet rewarding task endures of "[being] kind to one another, tenderhearted, forgiving one another, as God in Christ forgave you" (Ephesians 4:32). When the Small Catechism teaches that Holy Baptism is a daily drowning of the Old Adam—our internal sinner bent against sorrow for sin and forgiveness toward others—we should note a key word: *daily*. As in every day, for the rest of our lives.

Stuck in Sin but Not Alone

Ponder this situation: Ken and Sue were approaching two decades of marriage. Amazingly for them, their arguments hearkened back to their earliest days together. The felt stuck. Sometimes in more tender moments with each other they would actually use that word. Stuck. The very saying of it seemed to accent its literal meaning. Stuck. Like an old 33-rpm record, life seemed to be an endless loop of argument, recovery, status quo, and failure. Their marriage, they thought, was irreparably scratched, even if they were still committed to sticking it out with each other. Their wedding vows mattered. "Until death do us part" were words that had sustaining value.

Beyond this, they both thought their marriage was substantially better than what they saw among their friends. Judy and Tom across the street had both been divorced once. Based on how the two of them talked with each other at neighborhood picnics, a second divorce was probably not far off on the horizon. Jack and Rachel at church barely sat next to each other on the same pew, opting more often for their kids to be human shields between them while they put in the time in worship—or so Ken and Sue concluded. Still, for Ken and Sue their argumentative monthly up-and-down experience exhausted them, sapping them of trust for each other.

Typically, their arguments followed a specific path. First came the offense. Usually minor and often able to be ignored under most circumstances. However, human nature being what it is, even minor offenses on certain days become major pains in the neck. Next came the confronting of that offense, usually in a somewhat ill-conceived way, sometimes downright thoughtlessly. Within minutes one or both of them were "in it to win it," bringing up a previous offense, sometimes an offense more than a decade old. Then came the "You always"/"You never" analysis, followed by Sue crying and Ken on the couch watching sports. After a few hours—which had lately become a couple days because this part of the timeline varied dramatically in proportion to the heat of the argument—Ken and Sue would find a way back to each other, apologize, and try to make amends. This pattern usually worked, and household harmony prevailed for a while until the next offense came.

Both Sue and Ken worried that such up-and-down experiences weren't normal. They assumed the majority of other couples were nothing like them. By allowing this thought pattern to proceed unabated, Ken and Sue forgot the fundamental truths about their identity. Created with purpose by God, they were corrupted by sin's lifelong power. In Christ that power would be broken, but the death throes of such inborn evil will be felt until our entrance into eternal glory.

This Christian couple forgot that the central expression of God's being is the person and work of Jesus Christ. To know God most is to know Christ best. As biblically faithful theologians put it, "The study of God is always first the study of Jesus Christ." In other words, "Don't forget Jesus . . . ever." For our purposes, "Don't forget Jesus in the middle of a marital dispute." By forgetting the significance of Christ's coming, the destruction of sin's power, Ken and Sue lived in state of constant vulnerability to the old evil foe we are told "prowls around like a roaring lion, seeking someone to devour." The constant calling for every Christian, but in this context, especially for married ones, is to "resist him, firm in your faith, knowing that the same kinds of suffering are being experienced by your brotherhood throughout the world" (1 Peter 5:8–9).

Did you read those words? Wow! Talk about a helpful marriage encounter—God's Word impacting your marriage with the truth that you are not alone. That friction, faction, and schism with your spouse is not unique to your marriage. Every marriage is a struggle between two sinful human beings trying to live as God's redeemed children. Contrary to personal belief, Ken and Sue and most of us clearly reside in a more normal range of marriage experience.

Barking and Biting

Over the course of a lifetime together, most couples figure out their best approach to resolving conflict. In my premarital counseling as a pastor, I have referenced two very different kinds of dogs to help couples appreciate different ways of resolving conflict. Those dogs are Chihuahuas and bloodhounds. Every family has a method for resolving conflict that gets imprinted on each child as they grow. Some of these blueprints are healthy. Some are not so much. Regardless of whether the blueprint itself is healthy or not, the fact remains that two sinful human beings are the ones who are enacting those methods.

Chihuahua dogs, in my humble opinion, are yippy, snippy, whippy dogs. Put several of them in a cage and I envision many quick but frequent fights before harmony is reestablished. (Disclaimer for sensitive Chihuahua owners: I am sure this is an exaggeration of your dog's temperament; I use it only for illustrative purposes.) These kinds of Chihuahua-sourced arguments can feel violent, even if no physical or verbal abuse takes place. The spontaneity of the conflict is itself unsettling enough.

For others, the experience of conflict may appear like bloodhounds who happily loll on the front porch for days on end until something breaks the routine to such a degree the rising frustration can no longer be tolerated. These arguments are unsettling as well because of the number of offenses that have been stored up and come out in a rush, usually without much logical connection or easy resolution.

While you can quickly become exhausted and overwhelmed with words, emotions, and confused explanations of the real problem, the good thing in these situations is that people can rest from arguing for a long period of time. Unfortunately, dread over the intensity of the next blowup can be suffocating for a marriage and the tender souls that constitute it. For spouses who come from Chihuahua families who are always snipping but never to the level of ferocity like I just described, a bloodhound kind of response can mean instant death to the relationship. The fear of hitting that emotional tripwire can be suffocating for such a soul.

Drawing on the thrust of the last chapter, different personalities engage and experience conflict differently. When sin has been committed and real offense cast toward another person, the experience is anything but robotic. Quiet people deal with offense, real sin, differently than outgoing people. Part of honoring the unique creation that is your spouse or kids or parents or other relative involves taking into account the unique way his or her personality deals with offense—both the act of offending someone and the receptivity toward correction and reconciliation efforts. We're not just dealing with a checklist. Human beings are messy and made messier because of sin. Awareness of these differing personality nuances is important as we move forward discussing repentance and forgiveness.

To be clear, resolving a conflict, if only temporarily, is one thing. Requesting and receiving forgiveness is another.

Harmony can be established functionally. The focus of this chapter remains the deep-seated character-building quality of mercy and forgiveness. There are many marriages that function. Only marriages built on the foundation of forgiveness, given and received, truly thrive. Let's return now to some of the realizations by which strong families live.

Expecting the Imperfect

Strong families understand that one's ability to forgive does not come fully honed when you arrive at the altar as a bride or a groom. Realistically, the strongest couples who present themselves to God for marriage are those who know that they are bound to mess up. This is a matter of realistic expectations. These couples live by the creed that "all have sinned and fall short of the glory of God" (Romans 3:23). Each one's status in this world is constant fallenness. Self-authored escape is impossible from original sin, the sin from which all our actual Ten Commandment–violating sins originate. *Lutheran Service Book* invites us to confess, "We are by nature sinful and unclean" (p. 151). Whether Christian or not, escaping our nature by our own efforts is impossible. A couple who enters marriage expecting to experience the consequences of our sinful status start life together in the strongest possible place spiritually.

Ryan and Taylor were unpacking their first apartment together. The wedding was magical. Taylor's mother had done a magnificent job managing just about everything . . . in the most tolerable of ways! The gifts they received now lay scattered on end tables and chairs. A pile near the door marked the ones that would soon be returned for much needed cash. Of all the things they had, what they most obviously lacked was their first bona fide argument as a married couple. This did not concern them though.

You see, during their engagement they had spent time with their pastor talking extensively about what a marriage involving two sinful human looks like. They'd talked about the selfishness by which sin gets expressed in thought, word, and deed. Expectations were tempered. The fanciful notion that Ryan and Taylor had found in each other the perfect match that would fill every single moment with joy was completely demolished. Instead, the pastor had led them through a few select Bible passages in which even the apostles, the firsthand followers of God's Son, acknowledged their own shortcomings.

Ryan and Taylor learned that sometimes a Christian husband, because of sin living in him, will "not do the good I want, but the evil I do not want is what I keep on doing" (Romans 7:19). Sometimes a Christian wife will "have the desire to do what is right, but not the ability to carry it out" (v. 18). Both of them on various days of their marriage will show clearly that "sin . . . dwells within" (v. 20). When they apologize later, they may acknowledge a complete inability to "understand [their] own actions" (v. 15). And yet, in His eternal brilliance, God ordains that marriage after Adam and Eve's fall into sin is still good, still a worthwhile pursuit. Instead of despairing of what awaited them, Ryan and Taylor felt better prepared than they could imagine.

Their pastor reminded these two lovebirds that the starting point for forgiving each other was to receive by faith the forgiveness that God offered them in Christ. This is important to understand. In His work of forgiveness, Jesus Christ justifies us. By the power of the Holy Spirit, the power of sin is broken through our faith in the Gospel of Jesus as the atoning sacrifice for sin. With renewed hearts and souls we cooperate with Christ's work to quash the sinful actions arising from our flesh. Yet, as long as we live, that sinful nature will thrash and kick and yell and scream with every intention of making us slaves to it again. So, Christ forgives us, but the power of sin, though broken, still rages. In this way God's grace is even more amazing, since He provides this declaration of forgiveness even though we will return again having fallen once more.

Neither Ryan and Taylor nor Sue and Ken before them had it all together when they got married. Regardless of starry-eyed, emotion-laden love, both couples were severely compromised human beings on their wedding day. This is our story too, because no couple, Christian or otherwise, has it all together at the start.

People entering second marriages may be especially aware of these faults. For smiles and sound advice on merging two families together, read *We're Not Blended—We're Pureed* (St. Louis: Concordia, 2011).

None of us have it all together in the mature years as husbands and wives. However, the more we grew with each other under the direction and grace of God's Word, we also grew in the "grace and knowledge of our Lord and Savior Jesus Christ" (2 Peter 3:18). Without losing the sense of adventure and joy that is Christian marriage, a strong family approaches the altar with a realistic set of expectations for what life will be like when laundry overflows the hamper and household expenses press up against household income.

Progress Means Patience—Not Perfection

Strong families take into account that the completely forgiving attitude we strive for is equally unattainable through a few short years together. This realization lies at the heart of Ken and Sue's story. Both understood, as most couples do, that marriage takes work. The reality check came several years down the road when they assumed their marriage engines would be firing harmoniously on all cylinders.

Ken and Sue presumed that after a few years either the need for forgiveness or the intensity of offense would diminish. In fact, just the opposite occurred. Over time, Ken and Sue found their ability to push each other's buttons and incisively critique the other to be more powerful than ever. This is an easy trap to fall into. Distance may make the heart grow fonder, but proximity allows the heart to act more destructively. In marriage, as in most long-term relationships, this is most certainly true.

Finally, every family must keep in mind that each person's work in this area of Christian character will never be complete during this earthly life. Knowing the truth of such a sentiment, the apostle Paul wrote about his struggle for holiness: "Not that I have already obtained this or am already perfect, but I press on to make it my own, because Christ Jesus has made me His own. . . . But one thing I do: forgetting what lies behind and straining forward to what lies ahead, I press on toward the goal for the prize of the upward call of God in Christ Jesus" (Philippians 3:12–14).

In other words, give yourself latitude to grow and change, to live and move and be yourself within the working will of God over the course of a lifetime. God's glory is not only found in the faithful believers flooding into the city whose center is the Lamb sitting upon the throne (Revelation 20). God's great glory is found here and now, in the simple faith that daily claims Christ as Savior and lives toward others by that same forgiving faith. Christ Jesus has made you His own and given such persevering faith as the cornerstone of your Christian experience!

Therefore we continue striving to keep faith with the faith. Forgiveness never yields for anything in this world. We show our mettle, the constitution of our character, in offering forgiveness to others. This rallying cry, this Christian currency, will continue to work itself out, often "with fear and trembling," being "sure of this, that He who began a good work in you will bring it to completion at the day of Jesus Christ" (Philippians 2:12; 1:6).

Repentance and forgiveness is a lifelong part of our daily devotion to Jesus Christ. Drawing on our heritage from Luther's Small Catechism, this daily drowning of the Old Adam, bent against sorrow for sin and forgiveness toward others, is just that: daily—as in every day for the rest of our lives. In other words, get used to saying, "I'm sorry." Even more, get used to saying, "I forgive you."

Just as this capacity to apologize and offer forgiveness is valuable for married couples, the same principles also apply to parents and children, brothers and sisters. The prime difference is that we usually have lower interpersonal expectations for these other relationships. Parents may assume their kids to be relatively perfect, but it doesn't take long to notice the lying habits of a four year-old or the snarky rebelliousness of a teenager. Two sisters sharing the proverbial bathroom will soon put to rest any notion that sin lives anywhere but your Christian home.

To this point we've tried to get used to the idea that repentance and forgiveness are necessary parts of any relationship, to blow up any hope that somehow our family or our marriage could avoid those spiritual activities. The idea that any of us can escape for one second from the need to repent of sin and seek another's forgiveness is lunacy. Our constant prayer is shaped by the hope that God will "Declare [us] innocent from hidden faults" (Psalm 19:12). Hidden faults are found in all of God's children. Unaddressed, they pose a seismic threat to our spiritual integrity, both personally and in our familial relationships.

The Real Deal
—Repenting, Apologizing, and Forgiving

Building on our discussion, let's go three steps further and talk about what makes for (1) real repentance, (2) a good apology, and (3) meaningful forgiveness.

Real repentance and sorrow for an offense means just that: real heartfelt sorrow. The vast majority of humankind lives life as socio-friends, not sociopaths. By God's great design, we are bent to be aware of other's emotions. When they cry, we get choked up. When the audience laughs, we likely laugh as well. Real repentance is little different. Repentance invites us to put ourselves honestly and, often, courageously in the heart and experience of the other, . . .

. . . like the wife who is silent because
of the overbearing tone of her husband;

. . . like the child who is silent in the face
of a raging parent;

. . . or like the sister who is sad because
that remark about thigh size really cut to the quick.

Relating emotionally to the one who seeks our apology matters. Humans are not robots moving at ninety-degree angles on a chessboard called life. They are real people created by God in His image who, when offended, grieve and hurt. Assimilating their heartache is never a futile endeavor for a fellow child of God.

With a heart full of true repentance, a good apology is one tethered to the goodness of God. Acknowledging the offense, an apologizer-in-chief appreciates first the goodness of God's character that has been transgressed in miniature through an offense to a fellow sinner. It is powerful to know that our sins carry double the weight of guilt. In violating the conscience of another created human being, we simultaneously violate the conscience and holy character of that human's Creator. A real Christian apology throbs with spoken sorrow to both beings.

When it comes to meaningful forgiveness, it's important to keep in mind what humans can justifiably be expected to do and what they can't. Only God can forgive sins fully. Every human heart can try to forgive, but that old sinful nature is still at work tearing down and shredding to pieces a complete pardon for sin. Only God can forget past transgression. Even when we struggle against it, the sinfully conditioned human mind is a steel trap that will hold on to the hurts of yesterday for years to come. Human beings are not God. Through the mercy and work of Christ, we are, however, God's children. With a Spirit that daily drowns that Old Adam, we can forgive and forgive and forgive with the same limitless abundance as our God and Father. While unable to forget, we can remember simultaneously that we have sinned an equally unforgettable amount of times. Together as the Body of Christ, whether at home or in a congregation, we press on to forgive and forget as best we can, to go to sleep and wake up again with new mercies for new days ahead.

Just as Joseph was prepared by God "to preserve . . . a remnant on earth, and to keep alive for you many survivors" (Genesis 45:7), you are sent to preserve your family through a similarly great deliverance. This deliverance is founded on Christ and empowered by the mighty Spirit of God. He dwells within you, leads you into all truth, and confirms this fact: you can embrace forgiveness without apology.

Key Points

- Strong families demonstrate increasing mastery of repentance and forgiveness.
- The capacity to repent and forgive is cultivated over a lifetime. All people and families remain sinful and need to continually repent and forgive others throughout their lives.
- Real repentance, a good apology, and meaningful forgiveness are all necessary steps in strengthening a family.

Discussion Questions

1. Whom have you been withholding forgiveness from or not confronting with a real sin committed against you? Which family member deserves a good apology from you for a past sin?
2. What is it about that offense, either given or received, that bears the greatest emotional weight? In other

words, how will you show an awareness of the emotional hurt caused by you or to you?

Action Items

1. Collaborate with your family members on the best way for each of you to ask and receive forgiveness. Work on a conflict resolution strategy that fits each person's personality.
2. Practice active listening, a communication technique that helps ensure we understand correctly the exact nature of the offense. Active listening requires us to ask clarifying questions and repeat or rephrase statements made to us. In doing this, we allow our family member to feel heard and honored in the hurt he or she feels. Note, this active listening doesn't require us to admit fault. Active listening ensures we are on the same page before moving to resolution.

I believe in the Holy Spirit, the holy Christian church, the communion of saints, the forgiveness of sins, the resurrection of the body, and the life everlasting. Amen.

> *What does this mean?*
>
> I believe . . . the Holy Spirit has called me by the Gospel, enlightened me with His gifts, sanctified and kept me in the true faith. In the same way He calls, gathers, enlightens, and sanctifies the whole Christian church on earth. . . . In this Christian church He daily and richly forgives all my sins and the sins of all believers. (Small Catechism, Third Article)

Strong families get up each morning with two things on their minds for the day ahead: how they will live their Christian faith and how they can encourage their fellow family members to do the same. A family is not just a collection of individuals who happen to live near one another. Rather, a family is a living, Spirit-breathing organism in which each part does its specific work while cheering on other parts of the family to do likewise. Robots do not qualify for family membership. Eating, breathing, feeling, thinking humans form families. Putting those physical, mental, and emotional capacities to good and godly use is our daily calling.

In many ways, this mission-forward value for families is a direct carryover from the last two chapters. In chapter 2 we celebrated the distinctive gifts and abilities God entrusts to each human being and calls forth from them over a lifetime. In chapter 3 we relished the forgiveness of sins found in Christ and the restorative power that forgiveness affords our souls. Now, as uniquely gifted and forgiven human beings, we take a look at how the twofold blessing of families encompasses a third aspect: the vocational call to serve others as we have opportunity every moment of every day. This is the benefit of using the Creed as our governing structure for appreciating the Christian family. The threefold personality of God is a unified personality. All three persons of the Godhead conspire as one divine being with a singular divine will in our lives and the lives of others. Heady stuff, to be sure, but understandable enough for even young children to learn it in Luther's Small Catechism.

See a Need; Meet a Need

Abby sat eating her chocolate-flavored, highly processed corn puff cereal. Connor was screaming for cream cheese bagels. Lauren walked through the kitchen poking fun at everyone. Mom's blow-dryer was buzzing upstairs, and dad (me) sat listening to the morning news program. Mention is not made, except in passing, of the supersized Siamese cat, Phil, who stalked all five sets of ankles seeking a morsel of food before a long day of snoozing. The clock read 7:00 a.m. During the next forty-five minutes, the fur would start flying. The final countdown to loading up the cars and toddling off to our respective worksites had begun. First Abby would exit the building and drive to high school with neighborhood friends. Then, dad would hustle Lauren and Connor to get shoes on and make sure lunches got packed and stowed in backpacks. Usually at this point, dad would jump into the shower and get dressed. Mom would finalize her finishing touches for the workday. Three. Two. One. . . . Whoooooosh! Out the door we would all tumble. Only Phil would know existential peace for the next eight or so hours.

The morning routine for the Seidlers goes nearly like clockwork. Usually. As a pastor I know few families—even ones with just a single child—that experience precisely consistent morning routines. No morning takeoff from a family's runway occurs without a few birds clogging up its jet engines. At the same time, there is usually some rhyme or reason to the morning flow. The order siblings file in and out of the bathroom, how breakfast cleanup goes, the lunch-making regimens, even the appearance of sleepy-eyed family members emerging from their bedrooms—all these activities tend to take place with a regular cadence to them. Inadvertently rearrange this daily resurrection process and the possibility of nuclear family meltdown in our domestic reactor goes up exponentially! Proceed at your own risk.

One thing my family fails at often but is especially trying to improve at is our "see a need and meet a need" capacity in every moment of our day. The phrase is one that my wife,

Renee, and I picked up from our friend Craig Swenson when were church camp campers many years back. "See a need; meet a need" challenges us to always be watchful for opportunities to do good. Life is not to be navigated with blinders on. Christians watch for Christ's coming and the way in which Christ can come through us to others. The phrase also encourages. Literally. The goal is to be filled with a kind of courage all of us so often lack. Human beings are great at excuses and discovering every manner of reason for not doing good to others. The impulse of the Spirit's leading is clear, however. "If a brother or sister is poorly clothed and lacking in daily food, and one of you says to them, 'Go in peace, be warmed and filled,' without giving them the things needed for the body, what good is that?" (James 2:15–16). See a need? Meet it.

The memorable nature of this phrase makes it extremely portable and accessible, even by our five-year-old, Connor. Remembering, however, is the easy part. As Christ said at the conclusion to His Sermon on the Mount, "Everyone then who hears these words of Mine and does them will be like a wise man" (Matthew 7:24). Later, Jesus said, "Wisdom is justified by her deeds" (11:19). So also James says, "Be doers of the word, and not hearers only, deceiving yourselves" (James 1:22). Recalling the salad bar illustration in chapter 1, knowing what to do is one thing. Putting the call of the Spirit to practice is critical. It takes effort to revisit our motivation, skill set, social setting, and other environmental forces that affect our willingness to act. But all of those factors are in play when opportunity presents itself. Strong families work to live beyond aspiration. They do what many only hope to do.

Starting from our daily skeletons of faithfulness, putting follow-through meat on the bones of opportunity should be a key priority. Encouraging one another to do take the initiative when opportunity arises, and doing so ourselves in whatever vocation we find ourselves—this is the mountainous terrain by which our faith and faithfulness will be tested and approved. Remember as each day dawns that you do not begin it alone. Rather, just as at your Baptism, you begin each day in the name of the Father and of the Son and of the Holy Spirit. "If God is for us, who can be against us?" (Romans 8:31).

The Right Destination

"Earn a living." Seventeen-year-old Eric had spent the majority of his high school years with that phrase echoing between the hammer and anvil of his inner ear. His hardworking father impressed this on him almost daily as the ultimate goal of existence: "Earn a living." It was truly a noble goal, but was it the best goal?

What Eric heard from his father is little different from the messaging experienced by most of our kids: education leads to success, and the goal of life is to get a job. While stay-at-home moms and dads exist and in some places thrive, the media documents a world bent more on career-oriented achievement than any other personal life choice. Such workaday orientation is the key, we are cajoled to believe, to having success and a successful family. Successful families from this world's point of view and strong families biblically speaking are not the same. In fact, far from it.

Strong Christian families encourage faithfulness in whatever location they find themselves. On the other hand, successful families in the world's point of view see faithfulness only as the achievement of a particular goal. They see difficult circumstances as proof of failure rather than opportunities to forgive and be forgiven. To them, the journey doesn't matter, as long as the destination is reached—it's about doing whatever it takes to get there.

Biblical faithfulness is quite different. Families striving for this type of faithfulness are aiming for a destination, too, but it's a destination that isn't achieved by their accomplishments or improvements as a family. It's a destination given to them as a gift by Christ, who earned this for them. Let's try a metaphor (which like all metaphors eventually fail). It's like God has packed the family in the car to head to the perfect unending vacation. He's the driver. While what you do along the way can make things much more or less pleasant for everyone one else, it's not your job to drive or plan the route. No matter how much you bicker in the backseat, complain about the scenery, and refuse the healthy snacks He provides, as long as you don't reject the destination by jumping out of the vehicle, you're going to end up where God wants you to go. The destination that you reach through Jesus Christ alone is what matters most.

This isn't to say that faithfulness isn't found in every inch along life's road. It is. God is constantly giving us opportunities to love and care for one another. Every momentary chance to annoy someone, to complain, or to see them as an obstacle is a chance to appreciate, to compliment, to see the people we love as helpers, not hindrances. Helping family members see that minute-by-minute standard for judging faithfulness keeps a life properly aligned to the Creator, Redeemer, and Sanctifier of all people through faith in Jesus Christ.

Adding Value

"Add value to someone's life today." This encouragement introduces a different perspective to how most people understand the more common "Do unto others as you would have them do unto you" Golden Rule. It's tempting to see the Golden Rule as a karmic transaction—people anticipate getting to the degree they give. This interpretation is driven by greed and is dangerous because it leads to the conclusion that those who receive much good obviously deserve it and those who receive very little don't deserve any more. In contrast is the concept of your life as a channel for adding real value, centered in God and the salvation offered through His Son, Jesus Christ. This encouragement places the emphasis clearly on what is being given with no word yet on whether we'll receive a return on that investment. It reminds us of how God gave everything to us regardless of what we could or couldn't give in return.

Jillian didn't have the same social status as the other kids in her class. She played the same games and participated in sports and other extracurriculars, but often found herself on the low end of the social pecking order. Sophie lived on the other end of the social spectrum. She looked and played the part of an alpha girl yet did it with enough humility that parents liked her more than some of her classmates. Sophie's moment of truth came when she saw Jillian not fitting into a class activity. The environment was a crowded mess of people, and Jillian was getting lost in all the commotion. Sophie remembered the mantra, "Add value to someone's life today" and sprung into action. Truth be told, she was intuitively living out the end-times directive of our Lord: "Truly, I say to you, as you did it to one of the least of these My brothers, you did it to Me" (Matthew 25:40).

Jillian's mother was close by, keeping watch of her lamb, one who was precious in God's sight. She noticed Sophie step up and step in, making a difference other classmates failed to offer. Over dinner a few hours later, Sophie's mom shared with the family the phone call she'd received from Jillian's mom. With Sophie listening and blushing profusely, one mom shared another mother's joy about the grace that had been shown her daughter, Jillian. Sophie had no idea anyone was watching. What Sophie should really know is the reward contained in this verse: "But when you give to the needy, do not let your left hand know what your right hand is doing, so that your giving may be in secret. And your Father who sees in secret will reward you" (Matthew 6:3). With Sophie's two brothers and other sister listening, the family thanked God for these very opportunities to be the hands and feet and mouth of Jesus Christ, showing compassion to those who in this world are "harassed and helpless, like sheep without a shepherd" (9:36). A person can live with all the encouragement in the world. Taking the next step by taking the initiative is what really counts.

Extending Sophie's experience one more pace, take note that every child of God lives with purpose. Not just the able-bodied adult but also the feeble-bodied elder or the still-developing body of a child—every season of life affords its population the opportunity to make a difference in the lives of others. A good friend and former colleague was always quick to remind me and the congregation we served that our kids are not just the "church of tomorrow." These kids, from the youngest to the most almost-adult among them, are in fact the "church of today," with all the rights and burdens of responsibility that come with being sons and daughters of the King.

Prepared for the Unplanned

Life is not, however, a series of preplanned activities or set-in-stone routines. Flexibility is not the domain of just the flexible. Even the most type-A-personality, ducks-in-a-row, anticipate-all-contingencies kind of human being needs to confess, "My times are in Your hand" (Psalm 31:15). The proverb states clearly, "Many are the plans in the mind of a man, but it is the purpose of the LORD that will stand" (Proverbs 19:21). Wisdom of this depth and insight ought always to be kept close at hand. Consider these situations:

— You're at the coffee shop on your way to work when the barista doesn't greet you with the same upbeat smile, and there's no one next in line preventing you from asking, "How are you doing?"

— The teacher's aide took the time to send a note affirming your child's good behavior, and you have an opportunity the next time you drop off your kid to return the compliment.

— Your co-worker doesn't make a peep in meetings, but his red face expresses the pressure he's under on the way out the door. His exit from the room is your opportunity to enter into his life and help.

The opportunities to serve others are endless. They are as new every morning as the mercies of God that lift us out of bed. Tackling them as they come with verve and a sense of an adventure, along with an appropriate amount of apprehension, marks a strong Christian. That kind of engagement marks a strong family. Colored with a prayerful attitude, Christians can give evidence that "we have this treasure in jars of clay, to show that the surpassing power belongs to

God and not to us" (2 Corinthians 4:7).

Reviewing the experiences of Paul with the Corinthian family of believers may prove useful. If there ever was a church of chaos that pained the heart of this rather logically bent apostle, Corinth was that congregation. They possessed every material and cultural resource by which to dominate their local surroundings. Add to that the eternal power of the Gospel of Jesus Christ, and Corinth should have been the linchpin that held the Rome-ward ministry of Paul together. Alas, that was not to be.

The very resources they had were, through demonic influence, oriented away from the good purposes of God. Paul was flabbergasted by the chaos and immorality. Sexual, secular, and social sins were rampant. As much as Paul wanted to restore order to this factionalized congregation, the task would require great patience, a lot of ink and paper, and, most of all, the enabling work of the Holy Spirit. What became apparent to Paul when the congregation had finally been righted? The ability to do all this came from God, and it happened on a timeline set by the Lord.

We do not know what each day holds. We do, however, know the One who holds every day in His hands. And our lives rest in God's hands too. While not knowing the opportunities that lie ahead, we know that God has prepared us for them. Even the most uncertain and volatile moments can be navigated knowing God will prosper us and the work of our hands.

This reality confronted the disciples as they trudged with Christ ever-closer to the cross and a mission to be carried out without His physical presence shortly thereafter. Jesus Christ knew the days would grow long and the hearts of His followers would grow weary as the mission of the Early Church began. They would be rattled with fear and overcome with dread at the majesty of kings and rulers before whom they would testify. These disciples would announce God's grace and lordship over sin through the work of Jesus Christ, the King of all kings. One can only imagine the stirring hearts that attempted to figure out how to be faithful and confident while proclaiming Jesus to many who didn't want to hear. They knew that being faithful could (and did!) bring verbal and physical abuse.

Jesus had a simple and straightforward word to sustain them: "When [the antagonists of God] deliver you over, do not be anxious how you are to speak or what you are to say, for what you are to say will be given to you in that hour. For it is not you who speak, but the Spirit of your Father speaking through you" (Matthew 10:19–20). Remember: this is the promise of God to His followers as they give witness to hostile adversaries of God's kingdom. How much less frightening and more effective should it be for Christian witnesses to speak in settings where that antagonism is significantly less, where still-sinful hearts have already been softened by God's Law and repentant despair? In such a setting, any Christian should be prepared to successfully "make a defense to anyone who asks you for a reason for the hope that is in you; yet do it with gentleness and respect" (1 Peter 3:15).

With this flexibility we confidently receive each circumstance as an opportunity for our Spirit-sanctified soul to respond with courage and the gentleness of real Christian love for our neighbors. The opportunity may be with people we've known a long time or with a complete stranger who needs our help on a street corner. What is uncontestable is this: we are present in their lives at moments of need in which we have the resources to help them. All this is under the mysterious working of God's will that "for those who love God all things work together for good" (Romans 8:28).

God has fashioned you for noble purposes. Keep working while it is day for "night is coming, when no one can work" (John 9:4). Every moment is a God-given opportunity for you to show the character of the salvation afforded you by the Holy Spirit of God. Live it. Speak it. Show it. Walk it. "By [your] good conduct . . . show [your] works in the meekness of wisdom" (James 3:13). Most of all, as baptized bearer of the name of our triune God, realize that to this name "every knee should bow, in heaven and on earth and under the earth, and every tongue confess that Jesus Christ is Lord, to the glory of God the Father" (Philippians 2:10–11). If that is the response that God's name calls forth, then you know again that "in the Lord your labor is not in vain" (1 Corinthians 15:58). You can add this fuel to the family mission.

Key Points

- Strong families daily consider how to live their Christian faith and how to encourage each family member to do the same.
- Strong families encourage flexible and responsive faithful service in all places and at all times.
- Strong families view each moment as a gift from God and do not retreat from that God-given opportunity to show the love of Christ.

Discussion Questions

1. Of your family members, whose opportunities for service are most minimized or overlooked? the elderly, retired grandfather? the small, school-age child? the stay-at-home mom? How can each specific person's mission be affirmed and encouraged?
2. What part of your mission service to God is the hardest to sustain? a ministry to a hard-hearted co-worker? support for a chronically ill family member? What support can you identify and draw on from other family members so that you can persevere?

Action Items

1. At your family dinner table (or wherever you dine together), create a ritual of allowing, but not forcing, each person to share his or her "mission activity" for

the day. Celebrate successes and cooperate to overcome obstacles found in those activities.

2. Who is like you in church? Make the effort to find like-led Christians who follow God into mission locales of similar types. Working with your pastor or other church staff, create a fellowship group focused around a specific kind of service to others.

3. Help your child identify at the beginning of the day the opportunities for faithful service. Preparing him or her in advance for these opportunities increases the likelihood your child will actually serve others and grow with a built-in orientation to serving throughout his or her lifetime.

Effort is exhausting, regardless of what effort you are making. Effort depletes energy and wearies every part of one's being. As part of His creative work, God created the seventh day, the Sabbath day, as a day of rest. It was the first holiday, the first holy day dedicated to remembering God without interruption. While for most Christians the day set aside as a day of rest and a time to honor God is now observed on the eighth (or first) day, Sunday, it is not just to honor the Creator. For the Christian, the Sabbath honors the Redeemer and the Sanctifier as well. Sabbath rest is a creedal experience, an opportunity for us to celebrate our triune God as He has revealed Himself to us. In resting we reflect on God: the Father, the Son, and the Holy Spirit.

Strong families take seriously the need for physical, mental, and emotional rest. Good sleeping, exercise, and eating habits are essential so that the body, "a temple of the Holy Spirit within you" (1 Corinthians 6:19), is nourished and sustained. Low blood sugar, lack of sleep, and fatigue frustrate a person's mind and heart. It's hard to think clearly and have emotional energy when the body lacks vitality. No wonder the worst arguments in a marriage tend to occur at night, before bed, when a couple is the most physically exhausted and in need of rest.

Mental and emotional rest is essential for our minds and hearts to take a break from out-thinking and out-maneuvering other people. Sometimes we need to just close our eyes and stop engaging all the mental and emotional stimuli of the world. Any family counselor will tell you one of their most important habits is debriefing with other counselors the emotional burdens they carry that have been unloaded by patients in their sessions. We only have so much emotional shoulder before we find ourselves "heavy laden" and in need of "rest for our souls" (Matthew 11:28). Emotional weight gets magnified by our sin, by our need to control or save others from their plight apart from the help of God. Mentally, our minds simply tire out. Even graduate students find that physical exercise while studying for exams can provide that welcome respite from intellectual exertion.

Sometimes physical, emotional, and mental rest is a shared activity for families—taking a walk in the park on a sunny day to clear the mind or lounging at the beach. At other times, resting our body, heart, and mind involves individual effort, like sleeping or sitting quietly in the car without the radio on in order to decompress while coming home from work. Whether together or separately, resting the body and all the senses God gave us cannot be overstated. Rest is part of being a healthy human being.

For the strongest families, resting together and resting from one another spiritually are both critical. Spiritual rest in the arms of our Creator, Redeemer, and Sanctifier distinguishes a Christian's rest and recovery from the less-satisfying rest of all other people who dwell in this world. Let's consider what it means to rest in light of the three persons of the Godhead, both together as a family as well as individually. Resting together means worshiping God as a unit. This together-resting can include the hearing of one another's prayers, a harmonized voice, or a devotional thought spoken over a leisurely meal. Resting from one another entails just that: separation, solitude, and quiet. Even the most gregarious and talkative families benefit from some "alone time."

Resting with the Father entails returning to the comfort of knowing we are created. Together we reassure one another that God continues to supply and sustain our lives with His goodness and that we are not an accident of His craftsmanship. Individually, we delight in the most distinguishing aspects of our human identity, aspects no one could fully appreciate except ourselves alone and the God who made us. Resting with the Son means returning to the comfort of knowing we are redeemed. This goes beyond giving and receiving forgiveness among our family members to reminding them that they, too, receive forgiveness from our Father through Jesus Christ. Resting with the Spirit entails returning to the comfort of knowing we are set apart for good and godly purposes.

The rest of this chapter will revisit some of the friends we've encountered in past pages to see what particular kind of rest they might benefit from as individuals and families.

Worship Is Rest

Remember Jessica, Jacob, and Tyler? For them life was defined by their separate activities: Jessica and Jacob at work, Tyler at school and sports practice. Eventually, the time they spent together was defined by further managing the time they were apart. Who would run Tyler to this practice? When would Jessica get to the store? Did Jacob remember to tackle that house project before what remained of the weekend got away? The three were at home together for sure, but they might as well have been galaxies apart. Doing things near one another and being together are two entirely different activities. Life would be a lot more satisfying if the three of them could learn just one thing new to do together: rest in the worship of the Lord Jesus Christ.

Remember Alex and his siblings Alexa and Colin? Alex lived a life of pressurized achievement because of his parents. There was always something more to do. Truth be told, he spent a lot of time with his mom and dad. Many were the times when they had fun at the zoo or doing some other family activity. They even regularly attended church. Letting down anyone, much less God, was simply not an option for his family's DNA. Interestingly, even while at worship Alex didn't actually "worship." Rarely did his heart bend toward God in thankfulness for the bending of God's heart toward him. Alex was becoming like Christ's sad vision of the Pharisees: "These men honor me with their lips, but their hearts are far from me." Alex rested comfortably with his family. The learning curve he needed to navigate was how to rest well when it was just him, God's Word, and his heavenly Father.

Remember Haley and Diane? Discerning what the mother-daughter duo needed most presents a daunting task. On the one hand, you could argue the two of them needed to find common ground. Gathering together to create and sustain a pattern of shared rest and worship of their Savior would provide a useful base for working through their personality differences. What they share as baptized children of God could negate their respective points of personality that rub against one another. On the other hand, also as baptized children of God, they needed time to separately consider and relish what unites them.

Remember the chaotic Corinthians who vexed the apostle Paul? The recipe for their rest was a confusing stew of priorities. On the one hand, they were a congregation divided. Their worship life, the time when they were supposed to rest together and get rejuvenated for the work of ministry ahead—that corporate worship was a shambles. In order for them to reclaim their place in the Kingdom's advance, each of those Corinthians were challenged by Paul through many threats and pleadings to get right with God. Their most important activity of rest was to rest in the Law that momentarily burdened them with guilt and shame for self-absorbed behavior. However, their rest would not be complete, we know, until the mercy of Christ and the restoration of each member to the larger Body was complete. Chapter 14 of 1 Corinthians reminds us how ultimately important any body—and especially the Body of the Church—is beyond the multiplicity of individual members.

Remember David and Sarah, the problem solver and his wife from chapter 2? Whether together with his family or alone, David really owed it to everyone (himself, his family, and his Creator) to revisit the unique abilities that each member of his family had acquired over the years. The Davids of this world would benefit greatly by reflecting with deep thanksgiving on what their particular yet often-dominant talents afford problem situations and the people affected by them. At the same time, that deep reflective worship for the work of God the Creator should lead David and many others to an awareness that it takes many hands to make light work. Even the people affected by whatever problem may be at work have something to contribute. Leadership, hospitality, prayer, a word of wisdom or caution—all of these make for the healthiest solutions. Such solutions are hard to come by if one person in a family or group does not have the sensitivity to appreciate the potential contribution of others.

Remember Ken and Sue? The couple who really began to learn what forgiveness entailed after almost twenty years of marriage provides a lesson for all of us. Worshiping the Son of God, their Savior, as a couple would be a great activity for them. Listening to each other pray out loud, confessing sins committed against each other openly to God, would significantly change the dynamic of their marriage. No doubt obtaining a comfort level for this to happen would be molasses slow in coming. For both men and women, deeply bending your heart with another human being in confessional prayer to God does not come naturally. At the very least, making thoughtful, reverent congregational worship a weekly commitment would go a long way to breaking the weekly or monthly logjam of controversy that rhythmically swirled in Ken and Sue's marriage. In a sense, returning to our consideration of change in chapter 1, weekly worship is a structural change that Ken and Sue should ensure is sustainably present. There, and probably in the company of social supporters of their marriage as opposed to failing next-door neighbors, the outlook for their happiness would brighten considerably.

Remember the newlyweds, Ryan and Taylor. They were blessed with a pastor who assisted them in setting reasonable expectations for each other's behavior before their marriage officially began. As Ryan and Taylor grow in love and years, the avalanche of increasing responsibility will begin to fall on them. Kids will come. Promotions will be earned. Their home will probably get larger and with it their debt and other financial obligations. Keeping their focus on the One who brought them to this point of a mercy-filled marriage must be priority one. Maintaining a balance of personal devotions and worshiping at church together may not guarantee smooth sailing, for trials will certainly come. However, such a devotional consistency will tether them tightly to the cross so that when they find themselves adrift as a couple or as parents, they can reach by faith for the lifeline that God's Spirit will throw them, certain that "no one is able to snatch them out of the Father's hand" (John 10:29).

Remember seventeen-year-old Eric? His life was overshadowed by the droning encouragement of his father to "earn a living." For all the effort of his teenaged life, the one place where he needed to have effort expended on him was in worship. The worship rest most beneficial for Eric is the kind moderated by a warm and caring Christian pastor, filled with the Gospel of mercy. Eric owes it to himself to pay close attention to the words of hymns and songs and spiritual songs so that, by God's grace, he may experience the "peace of God, which surpasses all understanding" (Philippians 4:7).

Remember Sophie and Jillian? Sophie's future is all sparkles. She will probably make a great name for herself and influence many people in her life. The importance of living under the lordship of God the Father, who has blessed her with such talent, cannot be overstated. As sinful men and women, thinking highly of ourselves is part of our nature's disease. Great is the boasting of the tongue, we are told in James. Sophie's ability to rest in worship so that she can be a follower there and not the natural leader she is will go a long way toward making her an even greater, more sensitive and compassionate leader for the Lord.

Remembering my family, I pray that you take advantage of the unique opportunities available for you and your family. The leading of the Holy Spirit and active obedience to that leading provides many dimensions to our worship and Sabbath resting. Resting in the embrace of God's mercy, we ask for wisdom as we look forward to picking up a relationship in the coming week that we initiated in the previous one. Perhaps there is a point of missional faithfulness that we are stumbling over. In worship we have the grace of being renewed in God's Word, receiving insight and direction from His Spirit for days of faithfulness ahead. As fellow family members worship, each carries the burden of being a resource and encouragement for the others.

Receiving with a Giving Heart

I am reminded of a story about the experience and attitude we should bring to the receiving of the Lord's Supper, the body and blood of Christ for the forgiveness of our sins and the strengthening of our faith—by which gift God works to amend our sinful lives so we may live in faithfulness and holiness before Him. The one who shared the story basically said this:

> When I receive the body and the blood of Jesus Christ, I realize that the benefit I receive is something that I alone will not experience. Rather, because of the powerfully present Word tied to that bread and wine, I know the effects of the meal will overflow into the lives of my family members. When I go to the rail, then, I am not just going there thinking about why I need it.

> Instead I take in my heart each one of my family members, my spouse, my kids, my grandkids. I even take my neighbors and some of my co-workers. As I taste the wine and savor the bread, I pull up images of each one of them so as to remind myself that my God-given life is more than something to be lived for my own pleasure or self-satisfaction. No, I see the impact I have on each one of these people God has ordained to be in my life. I see their hopes and fears, I feel any sadness they may face or uncertainty that has come upon them. I see them for who they are: sinners like me in need of a Savior. And I pray for them, that the all-surpassing power of God now at work in me would overflow to them.

I don't know whether that depiction of how one man receives Communion hits home for you, but by it I hope that you begin to see that rest is necessary for us and for the families who depend on us for strength. This, too, is something you can do. Rest in the arms of God: Father, Son, and Holy Spirit.

Key Points

- Strong families take seriously the need for physical, emotional, and spiritual rest.
- Strong families value resting together and resting apart, as individuals.
- The greatest rest, together or individually, is spiritual

as families rest by faith in the mercy and forgiveness of God's Son. This grace covers all the sins we commit as sons and daughters of our triune God: Father, Son, and Holy Spirit.

Discussion Questions

1. How can you improve the regularity of your daily and weekly rest? Think in terms of physical, emotional, and spiritual rest.

2. How can you improve the depth of the spiritual rest you receive? This may include more regular church attendance, personal devotions and prayer, or fellowship with other Christians socially.

3. What rituals can you introduce with your family members so that your family can learn to rest together? What expectations can you introduce with your family so that individuals take more seriously the call to rest regularly?

Action Items

1. Attend Christian worship. For all the action steps possible, the foundation of each is regularly hearing God's Word and receiving the Lord's Supper for the forgiveness of sins.

2. Different personalities pray differently, even while all pray to their heavenly Father through our Lord Jesus

Christ. Determine times in the day when you can stop what you are doing and take five or ten minutes to reflect on what has transpired so far, the people you've seen and conversations you've had, and the places your family members are and the service they may be rendering to others. Pray for yourself and for them before returning to the raceway that is our daily life.

A Final Word about Prayer

As I told many friends about the invitation to write this book, a singular refrain of advice met my ears repeatedly: encourage families to pray more. By now you may have noticed the body of this book did not include a chapter dedicated to the topic of prayer. And with good reason. Praying and knowing what to pray for are two different things. This book is dedicated to resourcing your prayers, to increasing the reservoir of theology you draw on when you close your eyes and fold your hands.

You see, it is one thing to pray for a husband to change and become more loving, more thoughtful, or more present in your marriage. It is another thing to ask God for help in really understanding his personality, which is completely different from asking God to assist you in lovingly pointing out a personality flaw in him, which is completely different from seeking God's help in forgiving him once again when that flaw erupts and affects the whole family, which is different from praying for your husband as he leaves for work the next morning, character flaws and all, to be an asset for God's kingdom work and a witness to the mercy of Jesus Christ.

Likewise, it is one thing to pray for a teenager whose personality and entire being is blossoming forth, that with his or her whole strength, soul, mind, and heart he or she would love God and serve others, and it is another thing to ask God for the courage to enter that teenager's bedroom and apologize for your own thoughtless words back in the kitchen an hour ago, a prayer which is a necessary precursor to your final morning farewell where you'll remind your child to be the light of Christ in that locker room.

Prayer is not a means of grace. Prayer is a servant for the Word of God that penetrates our heart and gives birth to our faith. With prayer we "groan to the throne" (see Romans 8:22), empowered by the Spirit to struggle with God for ourselves and others with the vision that the people we pray for "may stand mature and fully assured in all the will of God" (Colossians 4:12). True, Paul calls for us to "pray without ceasing" (1 Thessalonians 5:17) and with much "prayer and supplication with thanksgiving let your requests be made known to God" (Philippians 4:6). All well and very good. But to have the guts and the engine that drives our prayer with greater focus—that's the hope of this little book.

In closing, think about how you pray for those closest to you. What are the unique aspects of their personalities that are an asset for you and the other members of your family? Take time to thank God—really thank God—for them and those traits. Do so frequently, out loud, and specifically. Let yourself hear the words your heart places in your mouth with great detail. In doing so, the critical voices in your head will have a double enemy. First, the silent voices that rail against a family member will compete with the spoken prayer of a godly man or woman. Second, the God of heaven and earth will hear your prayers, offered in faith, and attend to them as only a compassionate God and Father can. "If God is for us, who can be against us" (Romans 8:31) and those whom we embrace with our prayers?

At the heart of our Lord's Prayer stands the capacity to forgive: "Forgive us our trespasses as we forgive those who trespass against us." For all the ways and times we feel offended—and the far fewer moments true offense is given us—forgiveness cultivated in our heart is critical. Chapter 3 reminded us that forgiveness toward others is built on a robust experience of God's forgiveness toward us. Sinful as we are and bent toward self-centered living, we don't take the forgiving of others lightly. Offering forgiveness is hard work, groaning kind of work. Make sure the forgiveness you develop in your family is surrounded by many prayers for God to forgive you as much as you pray for the courage and strength to forgive others.

Finally, it is a big world out there. Some would add it's a big, BAD world. When family members scatter to different parts of a town or city, they take their lives into their own hands in a way much different from when they are safe in the confines of a home. God goes with them. However, what choices each family member makes in the countless thousands of opportunities for witness before he or she returns to the friendly confines of home requires prayer. Pray in the rooms your family members will occupy. Pray with the faces of those they will talk to firmly painted in your mind. Pray for the decisions that will confront them. Pray for the character it will take to be the hands and feet and mouth of Christ in this world—His Body, the Church, serving the world, given to lead people to His body and blood for the salvation of all people.

As a final thought, consider Martin Luther's encouragement to pray, taken from the Large Catechism:

> We need to know this: all our shelter and protection rest in prayer alone. . . . For what do you imagine has done such great things up til now? What has stopped or quelled the counsels, purposes, murder, and riot of our enemies, by which the devil thought he would crush us, together with the Gospel? It was the prayer of a few godly people standing in the middle like an iron wall for our side. (III 30–31)

Prayer aligned with God's character and His will expressed through the persons of the Father, the Son, and the Holy Spirit is a powerful force against which no weapon can stand. Pray, yes. Pray thoughtfully expressing the work of the triune God in your life and the lives of your family members.